Happy Valentine's Day to:

Color With Me!

Mommy & Me Cupid's Valentine Coloring Book

Mary Lou Brown
Sandy Mahony

LOVE

Love is in the Air
HAPPY VALENTINE'S DAY

Love

Dear,

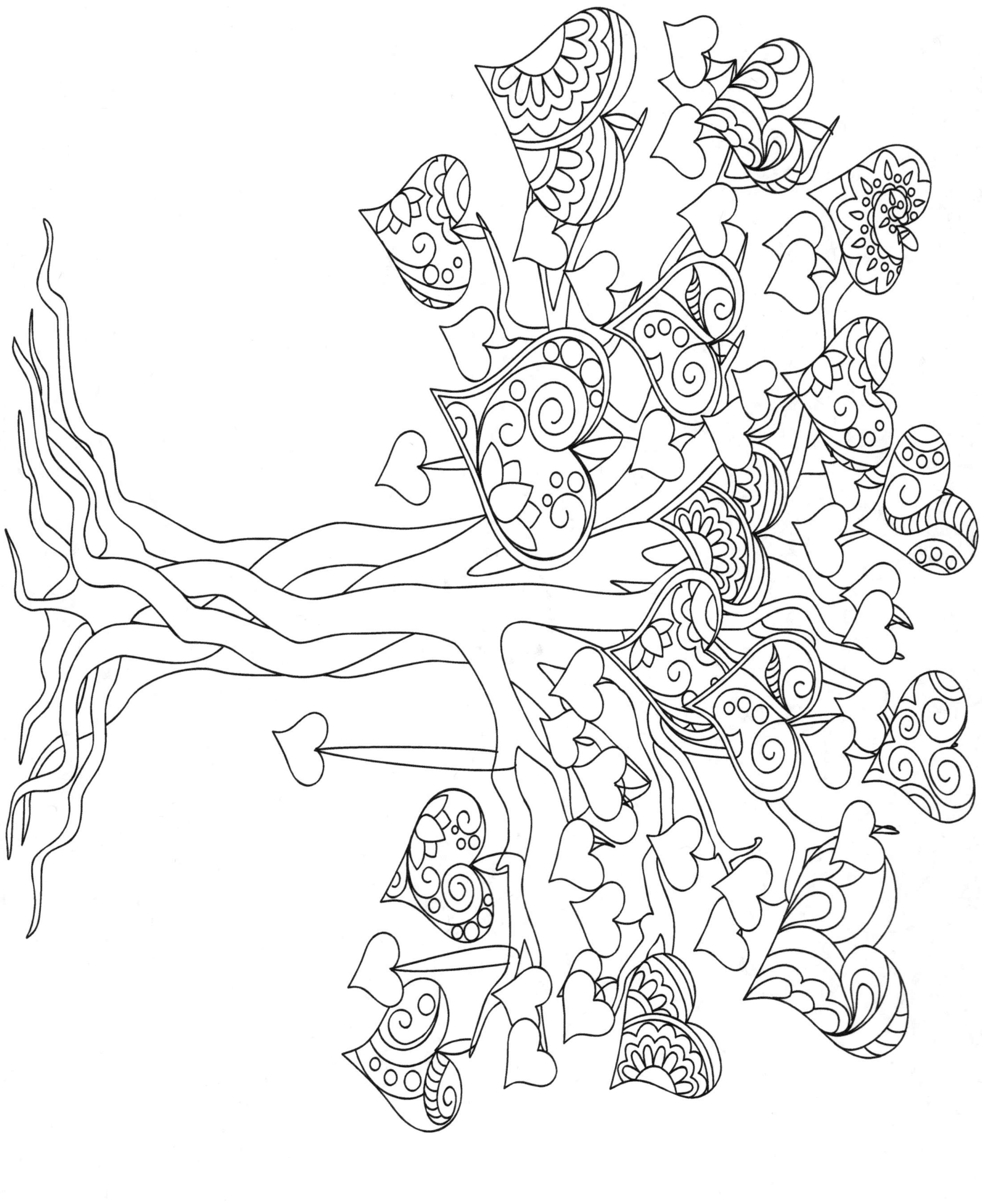

L♥ve
I♥U

HAPPY
Valentine's
DAY

I LOVE YOU

I ♥ YOU!

I LOVE YOU!
adventurelearningpress.com

www.ingramcontent.com/pod-product-compliance
Lightning Source LLC
Chambersburg PA
CBHW081414280526
45788CB00009B/3100
9781542418270